Horses Are Fun!

Mary Elizabeth Salzmann

Consulting Editor, Diane Craig, M.A./Reading Specialist

Sandcastle

An Imprint of Abdo Publishing
abdobooks.com

abdobooks.com

Published by Abdo Publishing, a division of ABDO, PO Box 398166, Minneapolis, Minnesota 55439. Copyright © 2022 by Abdo Consulting Group, Inc. International copyrights reserved in all countries. No part of this book may be reproduced in any form without written permission from the publisher. SandCastle™ is a trademark and logo of Abdo Publishing.

Printed in the United States of America, North Mankato, Minnesota

052021
092021

Design: Sarah DeYoung, Mighty Media, Inc.
Production: Mighty Media, Inc.
Cover Photograph: Shutterstock
Interior Photographs: Ella Herz, pp. 5 (paint), 21; iStockphoto, pp. 4 (middle bay), 17; Shutterstock, pp. 4, 5, 7, 9, 11, 13, 15, 19, 22

Library of Congress Control Number: 2019957510

Publisher's Cataloging-in-Publication Data
Names: Salzmann, Mary Elizabeth, author.
Title: Horses are fun! / by Mary Elizabeth Salzmann
Description: Minneapolis, Minnesota : Abdo Publishing, 2022 | Series: Pets are fun! | Includes online resources and index
Identifiers: ISBN 9781532193132 (lib. bdg.) | ISBN 9781098211776 (ebook)
Subjects: LCSH: Pets--Juvenile literature. | Horses--Juvenile literature. | Horses--Behavior--Juvenile literature. | Pets--Behavior--Juvenile literature.
Classification: DDC 636.08--dc23

SandCastle™ Level: Emerging

SandCastle™ books are created by a team of professional educators, reading specialists, and content developers around five essential components—phonemic awareness, phonics, vocabulary, text comprehension, and fluency—to assist young readers as they develop reading skills and strategies and increase their general knowledge. All books are written, reviewed, and leveled for guided reading and early reading intervention programs for use in shared, guided, and independent reading and writing activities to support a balanced approach to literacy instruction. The SandCastle™ series has four levels that correspond to early literacy development. The levels are provided to help teachers and parents select appropriate books for young readers.

EMERGING • BEGINNING • TRANSITIONAL • FLUENT

Contents

Horses Are Fun!

Can you find these pet horses in this book?

bay

pinto

palomino

paint

chestnut

A horse
can sleep.

A horse
can run.

A horse

can stand.

A horse

can drink.

A horse
can eat.

A horse

can walk.

A horse

can jump.

A horse

can pull.

What Else Did You See?

fence

grass

hay

water

Index

Teacher's Guide

ATOS: 0.5   GRL: A   Word Count: 32

High-Frequency Words

Content Words

drink, horse, pull, sleep, stand, walk

Before Reading

- Tell students that the title of the book is *Horses Are Fun!*
- Summarize the content of the book.
- Have students look through the book. Ask them what they see in the pictures.
- Choose a few new vocabulary words. Have students predict what letter each word starts with. Then have them find the words in the book.

After Reading

Ask students questions about the book's content, such as:

- Have you ever ridden or petted a horse? What was it like?
- Do you have a pet? What kind of pet is it?
- What other animals would you like to read about?